Quick & Easy
Freezer
Meals

pil

Publications
International, Ltd.

Pictured on the front cover: Baked Bean Stew *(page 42)*.

Pictured on the back cover (clockwise from top left): Egg and Sausage Breakfast Strudel *(page 60)*, Easy Chicken and Mushroom Stroganoff *(page 50)*, and Waffles *(page 10)*.

ISBN-13: 978-1-4127-1405-1
ISBN-10: 1-4127-1405-2

Manufactured in China.

8 7 6 5 4 3 2 1

Microwave Cooking: Microwave ovens vary in wattage. Use the cooking times as guidelines and check for doneness before adding more time.

CONTENTS

The Freezer Is Your Friend 6

De-stress your busy life by stocking your freezer with homemade meals

Breakfast on the Run 10

Raid the freezer to put this important meal on the table quickly

Skip the Sandwich 26

Stock a speedy lunch or light dinner in your freezer

Dinner in a Flash 42

Go beyond casseroles for make-ahead dinners

Freeze, Then Finish 60

Give your family something hot from the oven, fast

Build on the Basics 74

No room in the freezer? Just stock basics for quick meal prep

Index 93

Acknowledgments 94

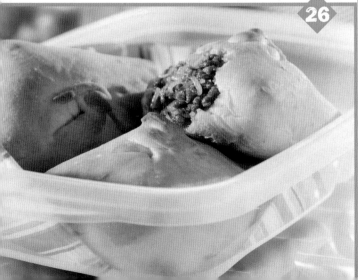

The FREEZER Is Your Friend

De-stress your busy life by stocking your freezer with homemade meals

Cooking for yourself and your family should be a pleasure, not a chore. But today's time pressures mean that meals often involve a phone call for a pizza, a quick trip to the fast-food drive-through, or the same two or three hastily prepared standards.

It doesn't have to be this way. You *can* provide varied and nutritious meals for your family during the week—just put your freezer to work. If you build up an "inventory" of frozen items (or at least the ingredients for fast combinations), you'll be able to put a meal on the table just as quickly as it takes to reheat it.

Using a stand-alone freezer allows you to prepare lots of different dishes in bulk quantities for the greatest number of choices. But even if you only have the freezer above the refrigerator, you can still store a respectable variety of made-ahead dishes.

Filling the freezer

You have several options when it comes to preparing dishes that will be frozen. Easiest of all is to double or triple recipes whenever you prepare a meal, and to freeze the extra portions to be reheated later on. If you package the extras in individual servings, you can even mix and match your meals to provide everyone in the family with their favorite dish.

When you have a little

more time to plan ahead, make larger batches of freezable foods on weekends. For example, make a large batch of pancakes, waffles, chili, stew, lasagna, or a favorite casserole. Then, fill your freezer containers to have ready-to-heat dishes that can supplement your daily meal preparations.

When there's a sale on beef or chicken, cook the meat ahead of time, then freeze it in smaller quantities for use in preparing quick dishes. For example, browned beef just needs some additional spices to turn it into a taco filling. Roasted or boiled chickens can provide cooked meat to use in crêpes, salads, or sandwiches.

If you do have a stand-alone freezer, you can prepare a month's worth of meals. By setting aside one weekend a month—one day to shop and chop, one day to cook and freeze—you can build an "inventory" of frozen meals that rivals anything you can find in the supermarket's freezer section. Best of all, your family can enjoy your home cooking, even if you don't have time to start a meal from scratch every day.

If you do cook in larger quantities, post a list on the freezer door showing the items you've placed inside. Then, as your family eats up your delicious cooking, just cross off the dishes you removed. When you notice your freezer "inventory" getting low, you can plan another cooking session, or start doubling up on your recipes again.

Protect your frozen foods

Your freezer can be an inhospitable place for food. Because cold air can't hold as much moisture as warm air, your freezer's atmosphere has a much lower humidity than the rest of your home. In fact, that low humidity is what enables freeze-drying to remove moisture from foods. But, unless you're freeze-drying food on purpose, you can wind up with undesirable freezer burn instead. So, you have to properly package dishes destined for the freezer.

You're probably familiar with your freezer packaging options:
- **resealable plastic freezer bags** (freezer bags are thicker and protect food better from potential freezer burn);

- **rigid heavy-duty plastic freezer containers** (square containers use available freezer space more efficiently than round or oval ones);
- **heavy-duty aluminum foil** (heavy-duty foil is thicker, to protect foods from freezer burn, as well as to resist punctures); and
- **heavy-duty waxed freezer paper** (use two layers for best protection; freezer papers laminated with plastic can be found in the same section as canning supplies).

To ensure that your foods come out of the freezer tasting as good as they went in, use only packaging specifically made for freezing. These heavy-duty items will protect the contents from drying out or absorbing odors from other foods, and they won't get brittle or crack at freezer temperatures. Whichever container you use, make sure that it's completely sealed; reinforce the cover or seams with freezer tape, if necessary.

Make sure you label the container with the name of the dish and the date you prepared it, using a grease pencil or marker pen. It's also useful to include reheating instructions, as well as any finishing instructions, such as adding grated cheese on top.

Maximize freezer space

Once you've prepared the dishes you plan to freeze, make sure they'll fit into the available freezer space. Don't freeze foods, such as rice, pasta, or noodles, that can be cooked while you reheat the rest of the meal—they'll only take up valuable space.

Try to use stackable rigid containers to make the most of your space. If you use plastic freezer bags, freeze the contents flat after squeezing out any excess air. Then, you can stack the bags more compactly, or even place them on edge to use skinny spaces. For dishes, such as casseroles, that need to be finished or reheated in baking pans, first line the pan with heavy-duty foil and cook as

directed. Once the dish is frozen in the pan, lift it out, wrap it in another layer of foil, and stack the frozen item on edge as well. Before reheating, remove the outer layer of foil, and return the frozen dish to its pan.

"Flash-freeze" smaller items, such as meatballs or bread rolls, by placing them on flat pans until frozen. Then, place the frozen items into freezer bags so you can remove only the amount you need. Cool larger dishes by placing the pot or pan in ice water; stir the contents when possible. Change the ice water often to quickly bring down the food temperature for safe packaging and faster freezing.

Foods that don't freeze well

In general, you can freeze just about anything if you prepare it carefully, package it correctly, and thaw or reheat it properly. Still, some foods don't freeze that well. Mayonnaise and sour cream can separate and appear curdled, and cream cheese can become watery after thawing, as can custard or cream fillings. Gravy also can curdle after thawing. Fried foods can become soggy, and greasy foods seem to get greasier after having been frozen. Potatoes might get mushy when cooked in a liquid, and mushrooms may darken; plan to add them to your dish later. You also might want to undercook pasta a bit, so it doesn't overcook when you reheat the dish. To freeze sandwiches, spread the bread with butter or margarine to prevent fillings from making the bread soggy when it thaws.

Not sure one of your favorite dishes will freeze well? Try freezing just one serving first. If it still looks and tastes good after you thaw or reheat it, add it to your freezer "inventory" when you make it again.

BREAKFAST
on the Run

Don't skip the first meal of the day—just open the freezer and you're good to go

Waffles

MAKES ABOUT 6 ROUND WAFFLES

2¼ cups all-purpose flour
2 tablespoons sugar
1 tablespoon baking powder

½ teaspoon salt
2 cups milk
2 eggs, beaten
¼ cup vegetable oil

1. Preheat waffle iron; grease lightly.

2. Sift flour, sugar, baking powder and salt in large bowl. Combine milk, eggs and oil in medium bowl. Stir liquid ingredients into dry ingredients until moistened.

3. For each waffle, pour about ¾ cup batter onto waffle iron. Close lid and bake until steaming stops.* Garnish as desired.

Check the manufacturer's directions for recommended amount of batter and baking time.

Preparation Tip: For crispier waffles, use less batter and let them cook for a few seconds longer after the steaming has stopped.

Freezer Note

Waffles can be prepared ahead and refrigerated or frozen in resealable plastic freezer bags. Reheat in toaster or toaster oven.

Baked French Toast Wedges

MAKES 6 SERVINGS

4 whole BAYS®
   English muffins,
   cut into 1-inch
   cubes

3 large eggs

½ cup sugar

1 teaspoon cinnamon

1 teaspoon vanilla

¼ teaspoon salt

1⅔ cups half-and-half,
   whipping cream
   or whole milk

2 tablespoons butter
   or margarine,
   melted

⅛ teaspoon nutmeg,
   preferably freshly
   grated

Spray 10-inch quiche dish or deep-dish pie plate with nonstick cooking spray. Arrange muffins in a single layer in dish. In a medium bowl, beat together eggs and combined sugar and cinnamon. Stir in vanilla and salt; mix well. Add half-and-half and melted butter or margarine, mixing well. Pour evenly over muffins; press down on muffins to moisten with liquid. Sprinkle nutmeg evenly over mixture. Cover and refrigerate overnight, if desired, or bake immediately.

Bake in 350°F oven for 40 to 45 minutes or until puffed and golden brown. Transfer to cooling rack; cool at least 10 minutes before serving. Cut into wedges and serve warm with desired fruit topping or heated maple syrup.

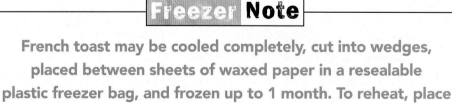

Freezer Note

French toast may be cooled completely, cut into wedges, placed between sheets of waxed paper in a resealable plastic freezer bag, and frozen up to 1 month. To reheat, place wedges on baking sheet and bake in 350°F oven for 8 to 10 minutes, or until thawed and heated through.

Mixed Fruit Topping: Combine 1 kiwifruit, peeled and diced, ½ cup fresh raspberries and 1 ripe small banana, sliced, with 2 tablespoons honey and 2 teaspoons fresh lime juice. Let stand 5 minutes.

Strawberry Topping: Combine 1¼ cups thinly sliced strawberries, ¼ cup strawberry jam or currant jelly and 1 teaspoon orange juice* in a microwave-safe bowl. Cover and cook at high power 1 minute or until warm. (Or, heat in a small saucepan over medium heat until warm.)

Peachy Keen Topping: Combine ¼ cup peach or apricot preserves and 1 tablespoon pineapple or apple juice.* Add 1 peeled and diced ripe peach or 1 cup diced thawed frozen sliced peaches and ¼ cup fresh or partially thawed frozen blueberries, mixing well. Serve at room temperature or heat as for Strawberry Topping above.

*Almond or orange-flavored liqueur may be substituted, if desired.

Silver Dollar Pancakes with Mixed Berry Topping

MAKES 28 (2-INCH) PANCAKES

1¼ cups all-purpose flour
2 tablespoons sugar
2 teaspoons baking soda
1½ cups buttermilk
½ cup EGG BEATERS®

3 tablespoons FLEISCHMANN'S® Original Margarine, melted, divided
Mixed Berry Topping (recipe follows)

In large bowl, combine flour, sugar and baking soda. Stir in buttermilk, Egg Beaters® and 2 tablespoons margarine just until blended.

Brush large nonstick griddle or skillet with some of remaining margarine; heat over medium-high heat. Using 1 heaping tablespoon batter for each pancake, spoon batter onto griddle. Cook until bubbly; turn and cook until lightly browned. Repeat with remaining batter, using remaining margarine as needed to make 28 pancakes. Serve hot with Mixed Berry Topping.

Mixed Berry Topping: In medium saucepan, over medium-low heat, combine 1 (12-ounce) package thawed frozen mixed berries,* ¼ cup honey and ½ teaspoon grated gingerroot (or ⅛ teaspoon ground ginger). Cook and stir just until hot and well blended. Serve over pancakes.

*Three cups mixed fresh berries can be substituted.

Freezer Note

Pancakes can be prepared ahead and refrigerated or frozen in resealable plastic freezer bags. Reheat in toaster oven.

Peachy Oat Bran Muffins

MAKES 12 MEDIUM MUFFINS

1½ cups oat bran
½ cup all-purpose flour
⅓ cup firmly packed brown sugar
2 teaspoons baking powder
1 teaspoon cinnamon
½ teaspoon salt
¾ cup lowfat milk

1 egg, beaten
¼ cup vegetable oil
1 can (15 ounces) DEL MONTE® LITE® Yellow Cling Sliced Peaches, drained and chopped
⅓ cup chopped walnuts
Granulated sugar (optional)

1. Preheat oven to 425°F. Combine oat bran, flour, brown sugar, baking powder, cinnamon and salt; mix well.

2. Combine milk, egg and oil. Add to dry ingredients; stir just enough to blend. Fold in fruit and nuts.

3. Fill greased muffin cups with batter. Sprinkle with granulated sugar, if desired.

4. Bake 20 to 25 minutes or until golden brown.

Freezer Note

Most muffins can easily be frozen. Wrap individually in plastic wrap and store in resealable plastic freezer bags. Reheat in microwave or toaster oven, or allow to thaw at room temperature.

Rise and Shine Sausage Oatmeal Cups

MAKES 12 SAUSAGE CUPS

Oatmeal Cups

1 pound BOB EVANS® Original Recipe Roll Sausage

⅔ cup quick or old-fashioned oats

¼ cup milk

1 egg white

1 tablespoon finely chopped onion

Filling

2 teaspoons butter

8 eggs, beaten

½ cup soft cream cheese (plain or herb)

¾ cup chopped seeded tomato, drained

2 tablespoons snipped fresh chives, fresh dill or green onion tops

Salt and black pepper to taste

Preheat oven to 350°F. To prepare oatmeal cups, combine sausage, oats, milk, egg white and onion in medium bowl. Divide mixture evenly among 12 muffin pan cups. Press mixture firmly on bottom and up sides to form hollow cups. Bake 12 to 15 minutes or until cooked through. Drain cups on paper towels and keep warm.

To prepare filling, melt butter in large skillet. Add eggs; cook, stirring frequently. When almost done, fold in remaining ingredients; cook until eggs reach desired doneness. Divide mixture evenly among sausage cups; serve hot. Refrigerate leftovers.

Freezer Note

Sausage cups can be prepared in advance and refrigerated overnight or frozen up to 1 month. Wrap individually in plastic wrap and store in resealable plastic freezer bag. Reheat when ready to fill.

Creamy Oatmeal

MAKES 4 SERVINGS

1⅓ cups uncooked old-fashioned oats
3 cups milk

½ cup raisins
4 teaspoons sugar
⅛ teaspoon salt

1. Combine oats, milk, raisins, sugar and salt in medium saucepan over medium heat.

2. Bring to a boil, stirring occasionally. Reduce heat and simmer 5 minutes. Cover; remove from heat. Let stand 5 minutes.

Freezer Note

For a quick, make-ahead breakfast, freeze oatmeal in individual portions. It can be reheated quickly in the microwave, saving the fuss of measuring, cooking, and cleaning up.

Homemade Sausage Patties

MAKES 16 SAUSAGE PATTIES

1½ pounds ground pork
½ pound ground turkey
2 teaspoons rubbed sage
1½ teaspoons salt

1 to 1½ teaspoons black pepper
1 teaspoon dried thyme leaves
½ teaspoon fennel seeds, crushed (optional)

Homemade
Sausage Patties

1. Combine pork, turkey, sage, salt, pepper, thyme and fennel seeds in large bowl; mix well. Cover and refrigerate at least 1 hour or up to 24 hours.

2. For each sausage patty, shape ¼ cup pork mixture into ½-inch-thick patty, about 2½ inches in diameter. Heat large skillet over medium-high heat until hot. Add as many sausage patties as will fit without crowding skillet. Cook sausage patties 4 minutes, turning halfway through cooking.

3. Reduce heat to medium-low and continue cooking sausage patties 6 to 8 minutes more or until no longer pink in center, turning halfway through cooking. Repeat with remaining sausage patties.

Freezer Note

Sausage patties can be frozen up to 1 month. Wrap individual patties in plastic wrap and store in resealable plastic freezer bags. Reheat in microwave or toaster oven.

Breakfast Cookies

MAKES 5 TO 6 DOZEN COOKIES

- 1 Butter Flavor CRISCO® Stick or 1 cup Butter Flavor CRISCO® all-vegetable shortening
- 1 cup JIF® Extra Crunchy Peanut Butter
- ¾ cup granulated sugar
- ¾ cup firmly packed brown sugar
- 2 eggs, beaten
- 1½ cups all-purpose flour
- 1 teaspoon baking powder
- 1 teaspoon baking soda
- 1 teaspoon ground cinnamon
- 1¾ cups quick oats, uncooked
- 1¼ cups raisins
- 1 medium Granny Smith apple, finely grated, including juice
- ⅓ cup finely grated carrot
- ¼ cup flake coconut (optional)

Preheat oven to 350°F. Place sheets of foil on countertop for cooling cookies.

Combine 1 cup shortening, JIF® peanut butter and sugars in large bowl. Beat at medium speed with electric mixer until blended. Beat in eggs.

Combine flour, baking powder, baking soda and cinnamon. Add gradually to creamed mixture at low speed. Beat until blended. Stir in oats, raisins, apple, carrot and coconut. Drop by tablespoonfuls onto ungreased baking sheet.

Bake for 9 to 11 minutes or until just browned around edges. Do not overbake. Cool 2 minutes on baking sheet. Remove cookies to foil to cool completely.

Freezer Note

Freeze cookies between sheets of waxed paper in resealable plastic freezer bag or freezer container with tight-fitting lid.

Oat and Apple Granola

MAKES 12 (½-CUP) SERVINGS

4 cups old-fashioned oats	1 tablespoon canola oil
½ cup sunflower seeds	¼ cup dried apples, diced
¼ teaspoon salt	¼ cup raisins
1 cup apple juice concentrate, thawed	¼ cup dried cranberries, blueberries or cherries
¼ cup honey	

Preheat oven to 350°F. Lightly oil a 15×10-inch jelly-roll pan.

In a large bowl, combine oats, sunflower seeds and salt. In a large measuring cup, blend apple juice concentrate, honey and canola oil. Drizzle liquid mixture over oat mixture and toss until evenly coated. Spread on prepared pan.

Bake 30 to 35 minutes, stirring every 5 minutes, until light golden and crisp. Transfer to large bowl. Add dried fruit and toss to mix. Cool completely. Store in tightly covered container for 1 week.

Favorite recipe from **Canada's Canola Industry**

Freezer Note

Granola can be stored in plastic freezer bags for up to 2 months.

Breakfast in a Cup

MAKES 12 SERVINGS

3 cups cooked rice	⅓ cup skim milk
1 cup (4 ounces) shredded Cheddar cheese, divided	2 eggs, beaten
1 can (4 ounces) diced green chilies	½ teaspoon ground cumin
1 jar (2 ounces) diced pimientos, drained	½ teaspoon salt
	½ teaspoon ground black pepper
	Vegetable cooking spray

Breakfast in a Cup

Combine rice, ½ cup cheese, chilies, pimientos, milk, eggs, cumin, salt and pepper in large bowl. Evenly divide mixture into 12 muffin cups coated with cooking spray. Sprinkle with remaining ½ cup cheese. Bake at 400°F. for 15 minutes or until set.

Favorite recipe from **USA Rice**

Freezer Note

To freeze breakfast cups, wrap individually in plastic wrap and store in a resealable plastic freezer bag or freezer container with tight-fitting lid. To reheat, microwave each cup on HIGH 1 minute.

Skip the

SANDWICH

Stock a speedy lunch or light dinner in your freezer

Meal in a Bun

MAKES 18 BUNS

2 **pounds frozen bread dough**
1 **recipe Tostado Filling or Pizza Filling (recipes follow)**

Thaw dough until warm. On lightly floured board, roll each 1-pound loaf into 12-inch square. Cut each into nine 4-inch square pieces. In center of each square, spoon 2 tablespoons filling. Pick up corners of each square and pinch together. Pinch each diagonal seam so edges are well sealed. Place on baking sheet coated with nonstick cooking spray. Bake at 400°F for 15 to 18 minutes. Serve warm.

Tostado Filling: Cook 1 pound extra-lean ground beef and ¼ cup minced onion over medium heat, until beef is no longer pink; drain thoroughly. Stir in 1 cup shredded Cheddar cheese, ½ cup tomato sauce and 1 package taco seasoning mix.

Pizza Filling: Cook 1 pound extra-lean ground beef and ¼ cup minced onion over medium heat until beef is no longer pink; drain thoroughly. Stir in ½ cup pizza sauce and 1 cup mozzarella cheese.

Speed it up: Substitute 2 cups of browned beef mixture (recipe on page 78) for the ground beef and onion in the recipes above.

Freezer Note

To freeze buns before baking, wrap individually in plastic wrap and store in resealable plastic freezer bag. To serve, place on baking sheet coated with nonstick cooking spray and bake at 350°F until browned, about 35 minutes. Leftovers may be frozen; to reheat, wrap in foil and heat at 350°F for 20 minutes or until hot in center.

Jamaican Meat Patties

MAKES 10 PATTIES

1 pound ground beef
1 onion, chopped
1 clove garlic, minced
¼ cup *Frank's® RedHot®* Original Cayenne Pepper Sauce
2¼ teaspoons curry powder, divided

1 teaspoon dried thyme leaves
1 egg, beaten
2 sheets folded refrigerated unbaked pie crusts (15-ounce package)

1. Cook beef, onion and garlic in nonstick skillet 5 minutes or until meat is browned, stirring to separate meat. Drain fat. Stir in *Frank's RedHot* Sauce, *½ cup water*, *2 teaspoons* curry powder and thyme. Cook 5 minutes or until liquid is evaporated, stirring often. Cool slightly. Mix egg with *1 tablespoon water* and remaining *¼ teaspoon* curry powder; set aside.

2. Preheat oven to 400°F. Roll out each pie crust sheet into slightly larger round on lightly floured board. Cut out 10 rounds using 5-inch cookie cutter, re-rolling scraps as necessary. Brush edge of rounds with some of egg mixture. Spoon about 3 tablespoons cooled meat mixture in center of each round. Fold rounds in half, pressing edges with floured fork to seal.

3. Place patties onto lightly greased baking sheets. Brush tops with remaining egg mixture. Bake 15 minutes or until crusts are crisp.

Variations: A small bowl measuring 5 inches across may be used for the cookie cutter. To make party-size appetizers, use a 3-inch round cutter.

Speed it up: Substitute 2 cups of browned beef mixture (recipe on page 78) for the ground beef, onion and garlic in the recipe above.

Freezer Note

Prepare ahead and freeze before baking; wrap securely in foil, and store in plastic freezer bag. Bake, uncovered, 15 minutes at 400°F.

Ham and Swiss Quiche

MAKES 8 SERVINGS

1 *unbaked* 9-inch (4-cup volume) deep-dish pie shell

1 cup (4 ounces) shredded Swiss cheese, divided

1 cup finely chopped cooked ham

2 green onions, sliced

1 can (12 fluid ounces) NESTLÉ® CARNATION® Evaporated Milk

3 large eggs

¼ cup all-purpose flour

¼ teaspoon salt

⅛ teaspoon ground black pepper

PREHEAT oven to 350°F.

SPRINKLE ½ *cup* cheese, ham and green onions into pie crust. Whisk together evaporated milk, eggs, flour, salt and pepper in large bowl. Pour mixture into pie shell; sprinkle with *remaining* cheese.

BAKE for 45 to 50 minutes or until knife inserted near center comes out clean. Cool on wire rack for 10 minutes before serving.

For Mini-Quiche Appetizers: Use 1½ packages (3 crusts) refrigerated pie crusts. Grease miniature muffin pans. Unfold crust on lightly floured surface. Cut fourteen 2½-inch circles from each crust. Press 1 circle of dough into bottom and up side of each cup. Repeat with *remaining* crusts. Combine cheese, ham, green onions, ⅔ cup (5-fluid-ounce can) evaporated milk, 2 eggs (lightly beaten), *2 tablespoons* flour, salt and pepper in large bowl; mix well. Spoon mixture into crusts, filling ¾ full. Bake in preheated 350°F. oven for 20 to 25 minutes or until crusts are golden brown. Cool slightly; lift quiche from cup with tip of knife. Serve warm or cool and freeze for later entertaining. Makes 3½ dozen.

Freezer Note

Quiche can be frozen up to one month. To freeze before
or after baking, place on tray and freeze until firm. Wrap with
heavy-duty aluminum foil or place in a resealable plastic freezer bag
and return to freezer. Do not thaw before baking or reheating. To
finish unbaked quiche, unwrap and bake at 350°F, allowing 10 to
20 minutes additional time. To reheat baked quiche, unwrap and
bake at 350°F oven for 20 to 25 minutes, or until heated through.

Chicken Nuggets with Barbecue Dipping Sauce

MAKES 8 SERVINGS

- 1 pound boneless skinless chicken breasts
- ¼ cup all-purpose flour
- ¼ teaspoon salt
  Dash black pepper
- 2 cups crushed reduced-fat baked cheese crackers

- 1 teaspoon dried oregano leaves
- 1 egg white
- 1 tablespoon water
- 3 tablespoons barbecue sauce
- 2 tablespoons all-fruit peach or apricot jam

1. Preheat oven to 400°F. Rinse chicken. Pat dry with paper towels. Cut into 40 (1-inch) pieces.

2. Place flour, salt and pepper in resealable plastic food storage bag. Combine cracker crumbs and oregano in shallow bowl. Whisk together egg white and water in small bowl.

3. Place 6 or 8 chicken pieces in bag with flour mixture; seal bag. Shake until chicken is well coated. Remove chicken from bag; shake off excess flour. Coat all sides of chicken pieces with egg white mixture. Roll in crumb mixture. Place in shallow baking pan. Repeat with remaining chicken pieces. Bake 10 to 13 minutes or until golden brown.

4. Meanwhile, combine barbecue sauce and jam in small saucepan. Cook and stir over low heat until heated through. (If freezing nuggets, do not prepare dipping sauce at this time.) Serve chicken nuggets with dipping sauce or follow directions for freezing and reheating.

Barbecue Dipping Sauce for Reheated Nuggets: For each serving, stir together about 1½ teaspoons barbecue sauce and ½ teaspoon jam in small microwavable dish. Microwave on HIGH 10 to 15 seconds or until hot.

Freezer Note

To freeze chicken nuggets, cool 5 minutes on baking sheet.
Wrap chicken in plastic wrap, making packages of 5 nuggets each.
Then, place individual packages in resealable plastic freezer bags
or freezer container with tight-fitting lid. To reheat nuggets,
preheat oven to 325°F. Unwrap nuggets. Place nuggets
on ungreased baking sheet. Bake for 13 to 15 minutes or until hot.
Or, place 4 to 5 nuggets on microwavable plate. Microwave on
DEFROST (30% power) 2½ to 3½ minutes or until hot, turning once.

Pizza Turnovers

MAKES 6 SERVINGS

5 ounces reduced-fat mild Italian bulk turkey sausage

½ cup prepared pizza sauce

1 package (10 ounces) refrigerated pizza dough

⅓ cup shredded reduced-fat Italian cheese blend (10 ounces)

1. Preheat oven to 425°F. Cook sausage in nonstick saucepan until browned, stirring with spoon to break up meat. Drain fat. Add pizza sauce. Cook and stir until hot.

2. Spray baking sheet with nonstick olive oil cooking spray. Unroll pizza dough onto baking sheet. Pat into 12×8-inch rectangle. Cut into 6 (4×4-inch) squares. Divide sausage mixture evenly among squares. Sprinkle with cheese. Lift one corner of each square and fold over filling to opposite corner, making triangle. Press edges with tines of fork to seal.

3. Bake 11 to 13 minutes or until golden brown. Serve immediately or follow directions for freezing and reheating.

Freezer Note

To freeze turnovers, transfer to wire rack to cool 30 minutes. Wrap individually in plastic wrap and place in resealable plastic freezer bag or freezer container with tight-fitting lid. To reheat, preheat oven to 400°F. Unwrap turnovers and place on ungreased baking pan. Cover loosely with foil. Bake 18 to 22 minutes or until hot. Or, place one turnover on a paper-towel-lined microwavable plate. Heat on DEFROST (30% power) 3 to 3½ minutes or until hot, turning once.

Skip the **SANDWICH**

Caribbean Chicken Quesadillas

MAKES 4 SERVINGS

2 cups shredded cooked chicken

¼ cup *Frank's® RedHot® Chile 'n Lime™* Hot Sauce

¼ teaspoon ground cinnamon

8 (8-inch) flour tortillas

2 cups shredded Monterey Jack cheese

½ cup thinly sliced green onion

1. Combine chicken, *Chile 'n Lime™* Hot Sauce and cinnamon in medium bowl.

2. Top 4 tortillas with cheese, green onion and chicken mixture, dividing evenly. Cover each with another tortilla, pressing down firmly.

3. Heat an electric grill pan until hot; coat with vegetable cooking spray. Cook quesadillas over medium heat about 2 to 3 minutes until golden, turning once. Cut into wedges to serve.

Speed it up: Use cooked chicken reserved from Crispy Roasted Chicken (recipe on page 86) or Classic Matzoh Ball Soup (recipe on page 90).

Freezer Note

Quesadillas can be frozen after being assembled. Wrap individually in plastic wrap and store in resealable plastic freezer bags. Thaw quesadillas before proceeding as directed.

Broccoli-Cheese Quesadillas

MAKES 4 SERVINGS

1 cup (4 ounces) shredded fat-free Cheddar cheese

½ cup finely chopped fresh broccoli

2 tablespoons picante sauce or salsa

4 (6- to 7-inch) corn or flour tortillas

1 teaspoon margarine, divided

1. Combine cheese, broccoli and picante sauce in small bowl; mix well.

2. Spoon ¼ of the cheese mixture onto 1 side of each tortilla; fold tortilla over filling.

3. Melt ½ teaspoon margarine in 10-inch nonstick skillet over medium heat. Add 2 quesadillas; cook about 2 minutes on each side or until tortillas are golden brown and cheese is melted. Repeat with remaining margarine and quesadillas. Cool completely.

Freezer Note

Refrigerate individually wrapped quesadillas up to 2 days or freeze up to 3 weeks; store in resealable plastic freezer bags.

Savory Onion Cheese Tart

MAKES 2 TARTS

1 envelope LIPTON®
  RECIPE SECRETS®
  Golden Onion Soup
  Mix
1 cup milk
1 egg, lightly beaten
½ teaspoon rosemary
  leaves

1 package (8 ounces)
  mozzarella cheese,
  shredded
1 package (15 ounces)
  refrigerated pie crusts
  for 2 (9-inch) crusts

In small bowl, thoroughly blend soup mix, milk, egg and rosemary. Stir in cheese. Freeze 1 hour or refrigerate at least 2 hours until mixture is slightly thickened and not runny.

Preheat oven to 375°F. On two aluminum-foil-lined baking sheets, unfold crusts. Fold crust edges over 1 inch to form rim. Brush, if desired, with 1 egg yolk beaten with 2 tablespoons water. Fill center of each prepared crust with ½ soup mixture; spread evenly to rim. Bake 25 minutes or until crusts are golden brown. To serve, cut into wedges.

Freezer Note

Tarts can be baked, then frozen. Simply wrap in heavy-duty aluminum foil; freeze. To reheat, unwrap and bake at 350°F until heated through.

Hearty Chili

MAKES ABOUT 8 CUPS

2 cans (15 ounces each) pinto beans

1 pound ground beef or turkey

1 onion, chopped

3 tablespoons Hearty Chili Seasoning Mix (recipe follows)

1 can (28 ounces) diced tomatoes, undrained

1 can (about 14 ounces) beef broth

1. Drain beans and rinse under cold running water.

2. Combine ground beef and onion in large saucepan. Cook over medium-high heat 6 minutes or until beef is no longer pink, stirring to crumble beef. Spoon off and discard any drippings.

3. Add seasoning mix to saucepan. Cook 1 minute, stirring frequently. Add beans, tomatoes with juice and beef broth; bring to a boil over high heat. Reduce heat to medium-low. Cover; simmer 30 minutes, stirring occasionally.

Speed it up: Substitute 2 cups of browned beef mixture (recipe on page 78) for the ground beef and onion in the recipe above.

Freezer Note

Refrigerate prepared chili for up to 3 days or freeze up to 1 month in freezer containers with tight-fitting lid or in resealable plastic freezer bags. If available, use frozen Beef Stock (recipe on page 57).

Hearty Chili Seasoning Mix

MAKES ABOUT 1 CUP

½ cup chili powder

¼ cup ground cumin

2 tablespoons garlic salt

2 tablespoons dried oregano leaves

2 teaspoons ground coriander

½ teaspoon ground red pepper

Combine all ingredients in small bowl. Store in airtight container at room temperature up to 3 months.

DINNER
in a Flash

Go beyond casseroles for make-ahead dinners

Baked Bean Stew

MAKES 8 SERVINGS

1 cup chopped onion

1 cup chopped green pepper

1 tablespoon vegetable oil

12 ounces boneless skinless chicken breast or tenders, cut into ½-inch pieces

2 cans (15 ounces each) low-sodium baked beans or pork and beans

1 can (15 ounces) low-sodium garbanzo beans or black-eyes or 1½ cups cooked dry-packaged garbanzo beans or black-eyes, rinsed, drained

1 can (14½ ounces) low-sodium diced tomatoes with roasted garlic, undrained

¾ teaspoon dried sage leaves

½ teaspoon ground cumin Salt and pepper, to taste

1. Cook onion and green pepper in oil in large saucepan until tender, 3 to 4 minutes. Add chicken and cook over medium heat until browned, 3 to 4 minutes.

2. Add beans, tomatoes, and herbs to saucepan; heat to boiling. Reduce heat and simmer, uncovered, 8 to 10 minutes. Season to taste with salt and pepper.

*Favorite recipe from **American Dry Bean Board***

California Chicken Pot Pies

MAKES 6 SERVINGS

1 (9-inch) folded refrigerated unbaked pie crust

1 can (10¾ ounces) condensed cream of chicken soup

1 cup half-and-half or milk

2 cups (10 ounces) cooked chicken, cut into ½-inch cubes

1 bag (16 ounces) California-style frozen vegetable combination, such as cauliflower, carrots and asparagus, thawed and drained*

1⅓ cups French's® French Fried Onions, divided

¼ teaspoon dried thyme leaves

½ cup (2 ounces) shredded Swiss cheese

Or, substitute any package of combination vegetables for California-style vegetables.

Preheat oven to 400°F. Roll out pie crust onto lightly floured board. Invert 10-ounce custard cup on top of crust. With sharp knife, trace around cup and cut out circle; prick several times with fork. Repeat 5 more times, rerolling scraps of pie crust as necessary. Cover; set crusts aside.

Combine soup and half-and-half in large bowl. Stir in chicken, vegetables, ⅔ cup French Fried Onions and thyme. Spoon mixture evenly into 6 (10-ounce) custard cups. Place filled cups on baking sheet. Place 1 crust over each cup. Bake, uncovered, 30 minutes or until crust is browned.

Sprinkle crusts with cheese; top with remaining ⅔ cup onions. Bake 1 minute or until onions are golden.

Variation: Filling may be baked in 9-inch pie plate. Top with uncut 9-inch pie crust. Bake at 400°F 35 minutes or until crust is golden. Top with cheese and remaining ⅔ cup onions. Bake 1 minute or until onions are golden.

Speed it up: Use cooked chicken reserved from Crispy Roasted Chicken (recipe on page 86) or Classic Matzoh Ball Soup (recipe on page 90).

Freezer Note

Pot pies may be prepared ahead, baked and frozen. Do not top with cheese and remaining onions before freezing. To reheat: Microwave individual pies in microwavable dishes on HIGH 5 minutes or until heated through. Top with remaining cheese and ⅔ cup onions. Microwave 1 minute or until onions are golden. Or, prepare pies as above. Do not bake. Cover; freeze. Bake at 400°F 40 minutes or until heated through and crust is golden. Top with cheese and remaining ⅔ cup onions. Bake 1 minute.

45

Stuffed Cabbage Rolls

MAKES 6 SERVINGS

¾ pound lean ground beef

½ cup chopped onion

1 cup cooked long-grain white rice

¼ teaspoon ground cinnamon

Salt-free herb seasoning (optional)

1 egg white

6 large cabbage leaves

1 can (14½ ounces) DEL MONTE® Stewed Tomatoes, No Salt Added with Onions, Celery & Green Peppers

1 can (15 ounces) DEL MONTE® Tomato Sauce (No Salt Added)

1. Brown meat and onion in large skillet over medium-high heat; drain. Add rice and cinnamon. Season with salt-free herb seasoning, if desired.

2. Remove from heat; stir in egg white. Pre-cook cabbage leaves 3 minutes in small amount of boiling water; drain. Divide meat mixture among cabbage leaves. Roll cabbage leaves loosely around meat mixture, allowing room for rice to swell. Secure with toothpicks.

3. Combine undrained tomatoes and tomato sauce in 4-quart saucepan; bring to boil. Reduce heat; add cabbage rolls. Simmer, uncovered, 30 minutes.

Speed it up: Substitute 1½ cups of browned beef mixture (recipe on page 78) for the ground beef and onion in the recipe above.

Stuffed Green Peppers

MAKES 6 SERVINGS

6 medium to large green bell peppers

1 pound BOB EVANS® Original Recipe Roll Sausage

2 cups tomato sauce

2 cups water

1 small onion, chopped

1 cup uncooked rice

Sliced green onion (optional)

Stuffed Green
Peppers

Preheat oven to 350°F. Slice off tops from peppers; scrape out centers to remove seeds and membranes. Combine all remaining ingredients except green onion in medium bowl; mix well. Evenly stuff peppers with sausage mixture. Place in lightly greased deep 3-quart casserole dish. Bake, covered, 20 minutes. Uncover; bake 5 to 10 minutes more or until peppers are fork-tender and filling is set. Garnish with green onion, if desired. Serve hot. Refrigerate leftovers.

Tip: For a pretty presentation, slice 6 small peppers lengthwise in half through stem; scrape out centers to remove seeds and membranes. Proceed as directed, serving 2 halves to each guest.

Serving Suggestion: Serve with mixed salad of carrot, radish and cucumber slices drizzled with a vinaigrette.

Freezer Note

Prepared filling can be frozen flat in resealable plastic freezer bags. Thaw in refrigerator before proceeding as directed.

Beef Enchiladas

MAKES 4 TO 6 SERVINGS

Red Chili Sauce (recipe on page 80)

1½ pounds boneless beef chuck shoulder, cut into 1-inch cubes

½ teaspoon salt

2 tablespoons vegetable oil

½ cup finely chopped white onion

¾ cup beef broth

¼ cup raisins

1 clove garlic, minced

½ teaspoon ground cloves

¼ teaspoon anise seeds, crushed

12 (6-inch) corn tortillas

1 cup (4 ounces) shredded mild Cheddar cheese

¾ cup sour cream

⅓ cup sliced pitted black olives

Basil sprig and tomato wedge for garnish

1. Prepare Red Chili Sauce (recipe on page 80).

2. Sprinkle beef with salt. Brown beef in batches in hot oil in large skillet over medium-high heat 10 to 12 minutes. Transfer to plate.

3. Reduce heat to medium. Add onion; cook and stir 4 minutes or until onion is soft. Return beef to skillet. Stir in broth, raisins, garlic, cloves, anise seeds and ¼ cup Red Chili Sauce. Bring to a boil over medium-high heat. Reduce heat to low. Cover and simmer 1½ to 2 hours until beef is very tender. Remove from heat. Using 2 forks, pull beef into coarse shreds in skillet.

4. Preheat oven to 375°F. Heat remaining Red Chili Sauce in medium skillet over medium heat until hot; remove from heat.

5. Dip 1 tortilla in sauce with tongs a few seconds until limp. Drain off excess sauce. Spread about 3 tablespoons meat filling down center of tortilla. Roll up; place in 13×9-inch baking dish. Repeat with remaining tortillas, sauce and meat filling. Pour remaining sauce over enchiladas. Sprinkle cheese over top.

6. Bake 25 minutes or until bubbly and cheese is melted. To serve, spoon sour cream down center of enchiladas. Sprinkle with olives. Garnish, if desired.

Freezer Note

Beef mixture can be frozen after step 3. Store in resealable plastic freezer bags. Thaw in refrigerator before proceeding as directed in step 4.

Easy Chicken and Mushroom Stroganoff

MAKES 4 SERVINGS

4 boneless, skinless chicken breast halves

2 tablespoons butter

2 tablespoons all-purpose flour

1 medium red onion, chopped

8 ounces mushrooms, quartered

1½ cups chicken broth

2 tablespoons prepared coarse-grain mustard

½ cup sour cream

3 tablespoons chopped fresh parsley

2 cups cooked egg noodles

In large nonstick frypan, melt butter over high heat. Place flour in pie pan; add chicken and turn to coat well. Place chicken in frypan and cook, turning about 5 minutes to brown well on both sides. Stir in onion, mushrooms and any remaining flour. Reduce heat to medium and cook, stirring, until onion is golden brown, about 5 minutes.

In small bowl, whisk together chicken broth and mustard. Pour mixture into frypan and stir. Bring to a boil; reduce heat and simmer about 5 minutes. Stir in sour cream and parsley; simmer for 2 additional minutes. Season with salt and pepper to taste.

Serve over egg noodles.

Favorite recipe from **National Chicken Council**

Freezer Note

To freeze, transfer stroganoff to plastic container with tight-fitting lid. Let cool, uncovered, for 20 minutes. Refrigerate, uncovered, until cold, about 30 minutes. Cover tightly and freeze until needed. To thaw, transfer from freezer to refrigerator 12 to 24 hours before needed. Reheat in large, covered frypan over medium-low heat. Bring to a simmer and cook about 5 minutes.

Swedish Meatballs

MAKES 5 TO 6 SERVINGS

1½ cups fresh bread crumbs
1 cup (½ pint) heavy cream
2 tablespoons butter or margarine, divided
1 small onion, chopped
1 pound ground beef
½ pound ground pork
3 tablespoons chopped fresh parsley, divided

1½ teaspoons salt
¼ teaspoon black pepper
¼ teaspoon ground allspice
1 cup beef broth
1 cup sour cream
1 tablespoon all-purpose flour

1. Combine bread crumbs and cream in small bowl; mix well. Let stand 10 minutes. Melt 1 tablespoon butter in large skillet over medium heat. Add onion. Cook and stir 5 minutes or until onion is tender. Combine beef, pork, bread crumb mixture, onion, 2 tablespoons parsley, salt, pepper and allspice in large bowl; mix well. Cover; refrigerate 1 hour.

2. Pat meat mixture into 1-inch-thick square on cutting board. Cut into 36 squares. Shape each square into a ball.* Melt remaining 1 tablespoon butter in same large skillet over medium heat. Add meatballs. Cook 10 minutes or until browned on all sides and no longer pink in centers. Remove meatballs from skillet; drain on paper towels.*

3. Drain drippings from skillet; discard. Pour broth into skillet. Heat over medium-high heat, stirring frequently and scraping up any browned bits. Reduce heat to low.

4. Combine sour cream and flour in small bowl; mix well. Stir sour cream mixture into broth mixture in skillet. Cook 5 minutes, stirring constantly. Do not boil. Add meatballs. Cook 5 minutes more. Sprinkle with remaining 1 tablespoon parsley. Garnish as desired.

*Meatballs can be frozen at either of these points.

To freeze meatballs quickly, place on cookie sheet or shallow pan; place in freezer 30 minutes to firm slightly. Remove from freezer; place in resealable plastic freezer bag and freeze completely. To prepare, thaw meatballs in refrigerator before proceeding as directed.

Cousin Arlene's Spaghetti Lasagna

MAKES 6 SERVINGS

8 ounces uncooked spaghetti or other thin pasta

1 tablespoon butter

1 clove garlic, finely chopped

2 pounds 90% lean ground beef

1 teaspoon granulated sugar

Salt and black pepper

2 cans (8 ounces each) tomato sauce

1 can (6 ounces) tomato paste

1 cup sour cream

1 package (3 ounces) cream cheese, softened

6 green onions, chopped

¼ cup grated Parmesan cheese

1. Preheat oven to 350°F. Cook spaghetti in large saucepan of salted boiling water until almost tender. Drain and set aside.

2. Melt butter in large skillet over medium heat. Add garlic; cook and stir 1 minute. Add ground beef and sugar; season with salt and pepper. Cook and stir until beef is no longer pink; drain fat. Add tomato sauce and tomato paste; simmer 20 minutes, stirring occasionally.

3. Meanwhile, beat sour cream and cream cheese in medium bowl until smooth. Add green onions; mix well.

4. Spread some meat sauce in 2-quart casserole to prevent noodles from sticking. Layer half of spaghetti, half of sour cream mixture and half of meat mixture. Repeat layers. Sprinkle Parmesan cheese over top. Bake 35 minutes or until heated through.

Speed it up: Substitute 4 cups of browned beef mixture (recipe on page 78) for the ground beef and garlic in the recipe above.

Freezer Note

This casserole can be frozen. Thaw in the refrigerator overnight, then let it come to room temperature before baking. Bake until heated through.

Beef and Pasta Soup

MAKES 5 SERVINGS

1 tablespoon vegetable oil

½ pound beef round steak, cut into ½-inch cubes

1 medium onion, chopped

3 cloves garlic, minced

4 cups Beef Stock (recipe follows) or canned beef broth

1 can (10¾ ounces) tomato purée

2 teaspoons dried Italian seasoning

2 bay leaves

1 package (9 ounces) frozen Italian green beans

½ cup uncooked orzo or rosamarina (rice-shaped pastas)

Salt

Lemon slices and fresh oregano for garnish

Freshly grated Parmesan cheese (optional)

French bread (optional)

1. Heat oil in 5-quart Dutch oven over medium-high heat; add beef, onion and garlic. Cook and stir until meat is crusty brown and onion is slightly tender.

2. Stir in Beef Stock, tomato purée, Italian seasoning and bay leaves. Bring to a boil over high heat. Reduce heat to medium-low; simmer, uncovered, 45 minutes.

3. Add beans and uncooked pasta. Bring to a boil over high heat. Simmer, uncovered, 8 minutes or until beans and pasta are tender, stirring frequently. Season with salt to taste.

4. Remove bay leaves. Ladle into bowls. Garnish, if desired. Serve with freshly grated Parmesan cheese and French bread, if desired.

Freezer Note

Soup can be frozen after step 2 in freezer containers with tight-fitting lids. After thawing, proceed as directed in step 3.

◆

Broth can be frozen in freezer containers for several months; measure in 1- or 2-cup portions for use in other recipes. Or, freeze broth in ice cube trays, pouring 1 fluid ounce into each section. Then, release cubes and store in resealable plastic freezer bag.

Beef Stock

MAKES ABOUT
1½ QUARTS STOCK

- 4 pounds meaty beef bones
- 2 large onions
- 2 large carrots, halved
- 4 ribs celery, halved
- 3½ quarts cold water, divided
- 8 sprigs parsley
- 2 bay leaves
- 1 teaspoon dried thyme leaves, crushed
- 6 black peppercorns
- 3 whole cloves

1. Preheat oven to 450°F. Rinse bones in cold water; arrange in large roasting pan.

2. To brown bones, place roasting pan with bones in oven for 30 minutes, turning once.

3. Trim tops and roots from onions, leaving most of the dried outer skin intact; cut into wedges.

4. Arrange onions, carrots and celery over bones. Roast 30 minutes more.*

5. Remove bones and vegetables from roasting pan and place in stockpot or 5-quart Dutch oven. Skim fat from roasting pan with spoon; discard fat.

6. To deglaze pan, pour in 2 cups water. Place pan over burners and cook over medium-high heat, scraping up brown bits and stirring constantly 2 to 3 minutes or until the mixture has reduced by about half. Transfer mixture to stockpot.

7. Add remaining 3 quarts water, parsley, bay leaves, thyme, peppercorns and cloves to stockpot. Bring to a boil over high heat. Reduce heat to medium-low; simmer, uncovered, 3 to 4 hours, skimming foam that rises to the top with large spoon.

8. Remove stock from heat and cool slightly. Remove large bones. Strain stock through large sieve or colander lined with several layers of damp cheesecloth, removing remaining bones and vegetables; discard bones and vegetables.

9. Use immediately or refrigerate stock in tightly covered container up to 2 days. To freeze, follow directions on previous page.

*For added zip, you may spread 3 ounces tomato paste over bones at this point. Roast an additional 15 minutes. Proceed as directed in step 5.

Make-Ahead Dill Chicken in Foil

MAKES 4 SERVINGS

8 chicken thighs, skinned

1 teaspoon salt

½ teaspoon ground black pepper

½ cup butter or margarine, melted

2 tablespoons lemon juice

1 teaspoon dried dill weed

Vegetable cooking spray

3 green onions, thinly sliced

1 cup thinly sliced carrots

6 ounces Swiss cheese, cut into 8 slices

Sprinkle chicken thighs with salt and pepper. Combine butter, lemon juice and dill in small bowl. Cut four 12-inch squares of heavy-duty foil; coat each with cooking spray. Place 1 tablespoon dill-butter sauce on center of each foil square; place 2 chicken thighs on sauce. Divide onion and carrot slices evenly over chicken. Top each with additional 1 tablespoon sauce and 1 slice cheese. Fold foil into packets, sealing securely. Label, date and freeze chicken until ready to bake.* To serve, place frozen foil packets in baking pan and bake at 400°F 1 hour or until fork can be inserted into chicken with ease and juices run clear, not pink.

Favorite recipe from **National Chicken Council**

*If serving immediately without freezing, place foil packets in baking pan and bake at 400°F 35 to 40 minutes or until fork can be inserted into chicken with ease and juices run clear, not pink.

Freezer **Note**

Chicken may be frozen for up to 9 months. For better freezer organization, place individual foil packets in resealable plastic freezer bag, and label and date bag.

FREEZE
Then Finish

Give your family something hot from the oven, fast

Egg and Sausage Breakfast Strudel

MAKES 10 STRUDELS

1 pound BOB EVANS® Original Recipe Roll Sausage

¾ cup finely grated Parmesan cheese

1 (10¾-ounce) can condensed cream of mushroom soup

2 hard-cooked eggs, cut into ¼-inch cubes

½ cup thinly sliced green onions

¼ cup chopped fresh parsley

1 (16-ounce) package frozen phyllo dough, thawed according to package directions

Butter-flavored nonstick cooking spray or ½ cup melted butter or margarine

Crumble and cook sausage in medium skillet until browned. Drain off any drippings; place in medium bowl. Add cheese, soup, eggs, green onions and parsley; stir gently until blended. Cover and chill at least 4 hours.

Preheat oven to 375°F. Layer 4 sheets of phyllo dough, coating each sheet with cooking spray or brushing with melted butter before stacking. Cut stack in half lengthwise. Shape ⅓ cup filling into log and place at bottom end of 1 stack. Fold in sides to cover filling; roll up phyllo dough and filling jelly-roll style. Seal edges and spray roll with cooking spray or brush with butter. Repeat with remaining phyllo dough and filling. Place rolls on ungreased baking sheet, seam sides down. Bake 15 to 20 minutes or until golden brown. Serve hot. Refrigerate leftovers.

Pecan Sticky Buns

MAKES 15 ROLLS

Dough

4½ to 5½ cups all-purpose
   flour, divided

½ cup granulated sugar

1½ teaspoons salt

2 packages active dry
   yeast

¾ cup warm milk
   (105° to 115°F)

½ cup warm water
   (105° to 115°F)

¼ cup (½ stick) margarine
   or butter, softened

2 eggs

Glaze

½ cup KARO® Light or
   Dark Corn Syrup

½ cup packed light brown
   sugar

¼ cup (½ stick) margarine
   or butter

1 cup pecans, coarsely
   chopped

Filling

½ cup firmly packed
   light brown sugar

1 teaspoon ground
   cinnamon

2 tablespoons margarine
   or butter, melted

1. For Dough: In large bowl, combine 2 cups flour, granulated sugar, salt and yeast. Stir in milk, water and softened margarine until blended. Stir in eggs and enough additional flour (about 2 cups) to make a soft dough. Knead on floured surface until smooth and elastic, about 8 minutes. Cover dough and let rest on floured surface 10 minutes.*

2. For Glaze: Meanwhile, in small saucepan over low heat, stir corn syrup, brown sugar and margarine until smooth. Pour into 13×9×2-inch baking pan. Sprinkle with pecans; set aside.

3. For Filling: Combine brown sugar and cinnamon; set aside. Roll dough to a 20×12-inch rectangle. Brush dough with 2 tablespoons melted margarine; sprinkle with brown sugar mixture. Starting from a long side, roll up jelly-roll fashion. Pinch seam to seal. Cut into 15 slices. Place cut side up in prepared pan. Cover tightly. Refrigerate 2 to 24 hours.

4. To bake, preheat oven to 375°F. Remove pan from refrigerator. Uncover pan and let stand at room temperature 10 minutes. Bake 28 to 30 minutes or until tops are browned. Invert onto serving tray. Serve warm or cool completely.

*To use frozen bread dough, omit ingredients for dough. Thaw two 1-pound loaves frozen bread dough in refrigerator overnight. In step 3, press loaves together and roll to a 20×12-inch rectangle; complete as recipe directs. To make frozen bread dough, see recipe on page 70.

Freezer Note

Sticky buns may be frozen before baking; overwrap pan in foil to seal well. When ready to prepare, first thaw sticky buns in refrigerator, then proceed as directed in step 4.

Then Finish

Pizza-Style Stuffed Potatoes

MAKES 4 SERVINGS

4 large baking potatoes, scrubbed

½ pound lean ground American lamb

⅓ cup finely chopped onion

⅓ cup chopped green bell pepper

¼ cup chopped mushrooms

2 teaspoons dried parsley flakes

2 teaspoons Italian seasoning

½ teaspoon garlic powder

½ cup plain nonfat yogurt

½ teaspoon salt

¼ teaspoon black pepper

1 cup (4 ounces) shredded reduced-fat mozzarella cheese, divided

½ cup pizza sauce

12 sliced black olives (optional)

2 tablespoons grated Parmesan cheese

Pierce potatoes several times with fork. Microwave on paper towel at HIGH 10 to 12 minutes or until potatoes are soft. Cool slightly.

Preheat oven to 400°F. Cook lamb in medium skillet over medium heat until no longer pink; drain. Add onion, bell pepper and mushrooms; microwave on HIGH 2 minutes. Stir in parsley, Italian seasoning and garlic powder.

Make lengthwise slit in each potato. Scoop out pulp leaving shells intact. Place pulp in medium bowl. Beat in yogurt, salt and black pepper. Add ⅔ cup mozzarella cheese and ground lamb mixture; mix until blended. Spoon mixture into potato shells. Top each potato with pizza sauce, remaining ⅓ cup mozzarella cheese, olives, if desired, and Parmesan cheese. Bake 20 minutes or until hot and bubbly.

Favorite recipe from **American Lamb Council**

 Freezer Note

Stuffed potatoes can be wrapped in foil and frozen before baking.
To serve, thaw in refrigerator and bake as directed.

Southwestern Turkey Empanadas

MAKES 18 APPETIZERS

¾ pound JENNIE-O TURKEY STORE® Deli Premium Seasoned Cracked Pepper Turkey Breast, diced

5 small red potatoes, cooked, minced

½ large onion, diced, sautéed until soft

1 cup corn niblets

6 ounces mozzarella cheese, shredded

⅓ cup sweet BBQ sauce

2 (about 17-ounce) boxes puff pastry sheets

Salt and pepper to taste

Egg yolk wash

Heat oven to 400°F. Combine JENNIE-O TURKEY STORE® Premium Seasoned Cracked Pepper Turkey Breast, potatoes, onion, corn and cheese in small bowl. Mix well. Stir in BBQ sauce just until moistened. Roll pastry sheets flat. Using 4- to 5-inch round cookie cutter, cut circles from dough, re-rolling scraps. Place 2 to 3 tablespoons filling in center of each pastry circle. Fold pastry over filling and crimp edges together with fork. Brush with egg wash. Poke 5 to 6 holes in top of each empanada, place on parchment-lined sheet pan and bake per package instructions, until golden. Serve hot.

Variations: Any variety of JENNIE-O TURKEY STORE® turkey breast can be used in this recipe. Add green or red pepper pieces to the filling. Use pie crust instead of puff pastry.

Freezer Note

These appetizers can be made ahead and frozen in resealable plastic freezer bags or freezer containers with tight-fitting lids. Egg wash when ready to bake. Add 5 to 6 minutes to bake time if frozen.

Mediterranean Microwave Meat Loaf

MAKES 4 SERVINGS

1 pound 90% lean ground beef

¼ pound Italian sausage, casings removed

½ cup dry bread crumbs

¼ cup grated Parmesan cheese

1 large egg

⅓ cup plus 2 tablespoons prepared pasta sauce, divided

2 tablespoons lemon juice, divided

½ teaspoon ground allspice

¼ teaspoon black pepper

1. Combine ground beef, sausage, bread crumbs, cheese, egg, ⅓ cup pasta sauce, 1 tablespoon lemon juice, allspice and pepper in large bowl. Mix until blended. Pat into ball. Place in 9-inch glass pie plate or shallow microwavable casserole dish 9 to 10 inches in diameter. Press into 7-inch circle.*

2. Microwave, lightly covered with paper towels, on HIGH 8 minutes. Pour off drippings. Meanwhile, combine 2 tablespoons pasta sauce and remaining 1 tablespoon lemon juice; spread over top of meat loaf. Microwave 3 to 5 minutes more or until meat loaf registers 160°F in center. Let stand 5 minutes before serving.

Meat loaf may be frozen at this point; overwrap with foil to seal well. To prepare, thaw in refrigerator before proceeding as directed.

Sausage Pinwheels

MAKES 48 PINWHEELS

2 cups biscuit mix
½ cup milk
¼ cup butter or margarine,
    melted

1 pound BOB EVANS®
    Original Recipe
    Roll Sausage

Combine biscuit mix, milk and butter in large bowl until blended. Refrigerate 30 minutes. Divide dough into two portions. Roll out one portion on floured surface to ⅛-inch-thick rectangle, about 10×7 inches. Spread with half the sausage. Roll lengthwise into long roll. Repeat with remaining dough and sausage. Place rolls in freezer until firm enough to cut easily. Preheat oven to 400°F. Cut rolls into thin slices. Place on baking sheets. Bake 15 minutes or until golden brown. Serve hot. Refrigerate leftovers.

 **Freezer Note**

This recipe may be doubled. Refreeze pinwheels after slicing. Wrap individual pinwheels in plastic wrap and store in resealable plastic freezer bags. To serve, thaw slices in refrigerator and bake.

Freezer Buttermilk Biscuits

MAKES 16 SERVINGS

3 cups all-purpose flour

1 tablespoon baking powder

1 tablespoon granulated sugar

1 teaspoon baking soda

½ teaspoon salt

⅔ cup shortening

1 cup buttermilk*

You can substitute soured fresh milk. To sour milk, place 1 tablespoon lemon juice plus enough milk to equal 1 cup in 2-cup measure. Stir; let stand 5 minutes before using.

1. Combine flour, baking powder, sugar, baking soda and salt in large bowl. Cut in shortening using pastry blender or 2 knives until mixture resembles fine crumbs. Stir buttermilk into flour mixture until mixture forms soft dough that leaves side of bowl.

2. Turn out dough onto well-floured surface. Knead 10 times; roll into 8-inch square. Cut dough into 16 (2-inch) squares.** Place squares on baking sheet lined with plastic wrap. Freeze about 3 hours or until firm. Remove squares and place in resealable plastic freezer bag or freezer container with tight-fitting lid. Freeze up to 1 month.

3. When ready to prepare, preheat oven to 400°F. Place frozen squares 1½ inches apart on ungreased baking sheets. Bake 20 to 25 minutes or until golden brown. Serve warm.

***To bake without freezing:** Preheat oven to 450°F. Place squares 1½ inches apart on ungreased baking sheets. Bake 10 to 12 minutes or until golden brown. Serve warm.*

Basic White Bread

MAKES 2 LOAVES

2 packages active dry
   yeast

2 tablespoons sugar

2 cups warm water
   (105° to 115°F)

6 to 6½ cups all-purpose
   flour, divided

½ cup nonfat dry milk
   powder

2 tablespoons shortening

2 teaspoons salt

1. Combine yeast, sugar and water in large bowl. Let stand 5 minutes or until bubbly.

2. Add 3 cups flour, milk powder, shortening and salt. Beat with electric mixer at low speed until blended. Increase speed to medium; beat 2 minutes. Stir in enough additional flour, about 3 cups, to make soft dough. Turn out onto lightly floured surface. Knead about 10 minutes, adding enough of remaining flour to make dough smooth and elastic.

3. Shape dough into ball; place in large greased bowl. Turn dough over so that top is greased. Cover with towel; let rise in warm, draft-free place about 1 hour or until doubled in size.

4. Punch down dough; knead on lightly floured surface 1 minute. Cover with towel; let rest 10 minutes.

5. Grease 2 (8½×4½-inch) loaf pans; set aside. Divide dough in half. Roll out half of dough into 12×8-inch rectangle with lightly floured rolling pin. Starting with 1 short side, roll up dough jelly-roll style. Pinch seam and ends to seal. Place loaf, seam side down, in prepared pan, tucking ends under. Repeat with remaining dough.

6. Cover and let rise in warm place 1 hour or until doubled in size.

7. Preheat oven to 375°F. Bake 30 to 35 minutes or until loaves are golden brown and sound hollow when tapped. Immediately remove from pans; cool completely on wire racks.

Freezer Note

To prepare frozen dough, mix and shape dough as directed in steps 1 through 5. Spray 2 sheets of plastic wrap with nonstick cooking spray. Cover dough with plastic wrap, greased side down. Freeze about 5 hours or until firm. Remove loaves from pans. Wrap frozen loaves securely in plastic wrap; place in resealable plastic freezer bags. Freeze up to 1 month. To bake loaves, unwrap and place in greased loaf pans. Cover with towel; let stand in warm place 4 to 5 hours or until loaves are thawed and doubled in bulk. Preheat oven to 375°F. Bake 40 to 45 minutes or until loaves are golden brown and sound hollow when tapped. Immediately remove from pans; cool completely on wire racks.

Freezer Rolls

MAKES ABOUT 2 DOZEN ROLLS

1¼ cups warm water (100° to 110°F)

2 envelopes FLEISCHMANN'S® Active Dry Yeast

½ cup sugar

½ cup warm milk (100° to 110°F)

⅓ cup butter or margarine, softened

1½ teaspoons salt

5½ to 6 cups all-purpose flour

2 large eggs

Place ½ cup warm water in large warm bowl. Sprinkle yeast over water; stir until dissolved. Add remaining ¾ cup warm water, sugar, warm milk, butter, salt and 2 cups flour. Beat 2 minutes at medium speed of electric mixer. Add eggs and ½ cup flour. Beat at high speed for 2 minutes. Stir in enough remaining flour to make soft dough. Turn out onto lightly floured surface. Knead until smooth and elastic, about 8 to 10 minutes. Cover with plastic wrap; let rest for 20 minutes.

Punch dough down. Shape into desired shapes for dinner rolls. Place on greased baking sheets. Cover with plastic wrap and foil, sealing well. Freeze up to 1 week.*

Once frozen, rolls may be placed in resealable plastic freezer bags.

When ready to prepare, remove rolls from freezer; unwrap and place on greased baking sheets. Cover; let rise in warm, draft-free place until doubled in size, about 1½ hours.

Bake at 350°F for 15 minutes or until done. Remove from baking sheets; cool on wire racks.

Shaping the Dough: Crescents: Divide dough in half. Roll each half into 14-inch circle. Cut each into 12 pie-shaped wedges. Roll up tightly from wide end. Curve ends slightly to form crescents. **Knots:** Divide dough into 24 equal pieces; roll each into 9-inch rope. Tie once loosely. **Coils:** Divide dough into 24 equal pieces; roll each into 9-inch rope. Coil each rope and tuck end under the coil. **Twists:** Divide dough into 24 equal pieces; roll each into 12-inch rope. Fold each rope in half and twist three to four times. Pinch ends to seal.

To bake without freezing: After shaping, let rise in warm, draft-free place until doubled in size, about 1 hour. Bake according to directions on previous page.

Build on the
BASICS

No room in the freezer?

Just stock basics for quick meal prep

Tortellini Bake Parmesano

MAKES 4 SERVINGS

1 package (12 ounces) fresh or frozen cheese tortellini or ravioli

½ pound lean ground beef

½ medium onion, finely chopped

2 cloves garlic, minced

½ teaspoon dried oregano, crushed

1 can (26 ounces) DEL MONTE® Chunky Spaghetti Sauce with Garlic & Herb

2 small zucchini, sliced

⅓ cup (about 1½ ounces) grated Parmesan cheese

1. Cook pasta according to package directions; rinse and drain.

2. Meanwhile, brown beef with onion, garlic and oregano in large skillet over medium-high heat; drain. Season with salt and pepper, if desired.

3. Add spaghetti sauce and zucchini. Cook 15 minutes or until thickened, stirring occasionally.

4. Arrange half of pasta in oiled 2-quart microwavable dish; top with half each of sauce and cheese. Repeat layers ending with cheese; cover.

5. Microwave on HIGH 8 to 10 minutes or until heated through, rotating dish halfway through cooking time.

Speed it up: Substitute 1 cup of browned beef mixture (recipe on page 78) for the ground beef and onion in the recipe above.

Freezer Note

For convenience, double the recipe and freeze one for later use. The recipe can also be made ahead, refrigerated and heated just before serving (allow extra time in microwave if dish is chilled).

Spaghetti Bolognese

MAKES 8 SERVINGS

1 pound lean ground beef
(or ½ pound ground
beef and ½ pound
bulk Italian sausage)

⅓ cup CRISCO® Oil,*
divided

½ pound mushrooms,
cleaned, stems
trimmed, and sliced

1 large onion, peeled
and diced

1 tablespoon jarred
minced garlic (or
2 large garlic cloves,
peeled and minced)

1 teaspoon salt, divided

1 teaspoon freshly ground
black pepper, divided

1 can (14½ ounces)
tomatoes packed
in tomato purée

1 can (8 ounces) tomato
paste

1 to 2 teaspoons Italian
herb seasoning

¾ pound spaghetti
Freshly grated Parmesan
cheese (optional)

*Use your favorite Crisco Oil
product.*

1. Heat large skillet on medium-high heat. Add beef. Break up lumps with fork. Cook 3 to 4 minutes, or until beef is no longer pink. Remove beef from pan with slotted spoon. Set aside. Discard drippings from pan.

2. Return skillet to medium-high heat. Add 3 tablespoons oil. Add mushrooms, onion and garlic. Sauté 2 minutes. Sprinkle with ½ teaspoon salt and ½ teaspoon pepper. Cook 3 minutes, or until onion is translucent.

3. Return beef to pan. Add tomatoes, tomato paste, Italian seasoning and remaining ½ teaspoon salt and remaining ½ teaspoon pepper. Bring to a boil. Reduce heat to low. Simmer sauce 30 to 40 minutes, or until it reaches desired consistency. Stir occasionally.

4. While sauce simmers, cook pasta in large pot of salted water with remaining oil, according to package directions. Drain. Top with sauce. Serve with cheese, if desired.

Speed it up: Substitute 2 cups of browned beef mixture (recipe on page 78) for the ground beef and onion in the recipe above.

Freezer Note

The sauce can be prepared up to 2 days in advance and refrigerated, tightly covered. Reheat it over low heat or in microwave oven; do not cook pasta until just before serving. For future dinners, you can make a double batch of this sauce and freeze half for up to three months.

Basic Browned Ground Beef

MAKES ABOUT 6 (2-CUP) PORTIONS

5 pounds lean ground beef

2¾ cups chopped celery

2¾ cups chopped onion

1 tablespoon minced garlic

1 teaspoon freshly ground black pepper

1 teaspoon salt (optional)

1. Brown beef in large stockpot, then drain excess fat.*

2. Add celery, onion, garlic, pepper and salt; cook and stir 1 minute. Cover pot and allow mixture to simmer 8 to 10 minutes, or until vegetables are tender-crisp.

3. Allow mixture to cool slightly, then place 1- or 2-cup portions into resealable plastic freezer bags. Freeze flat to conserve freezer space.

If you prefer, you can boil the ground beef instead. Bring water to a boil in a large stockpot. Add the ground beef; stir and continue boiling until the beef is cooked. Drain, reserving the cooking water for stock, if desired (skim excess fat off the top after cooling). Add the vegetables and proceed as directed.

Freezer Note

Freezing flat the browned beef in resealable plastic freezer bags also allows the mixture to thaw more quickly, either in the refrigerator or in a microwave oven.

Veg•All® Beef Chili

MAKES 6 TO 8 SERVINGS

- 1 can (28 ounces) tomato sauce
- 1 pound ground beef, browned and drained
- 1 can (16 ounces) kidney beans, drained and rinsed
- 1 can (15 ounces) VEG•ALL® Original Mixed Vegetables, with liquid
- 1 can (14½ ounces) whole tomatoes, cut up
- ¾ cup sliced green onions
- 2 teaspoons chili powder
- ¼ teaspoon black pepper
  Corn chips
  Shredded cheese
  Diced green onions

In 3-quart saucepan, combine all ingredients. Bring to a boil; reduce heat, cover, and simmer for 20 to 30 minutes, stirring occasionally. Serve hot with corn chips, shredded cheese, and diced green onions as toppers.

Note: A vegetarian version can be made by eliminating the ground beef and adding 1 teaspoon dried oregano and ½ teaspoon ground cumin.

Speed it up: Substitute 2 cups of browned beef mixture (recipe on page 78) for the ground beef in the recipe above.

Red Chili Sauce

MAKES ABOUT 2½ CUPS

3 ounces dried ancho chilies (about 5) seeded, deveined and rinsed

2½ cups boiling water

2 tablespoons vegetable oil

2 tablespoons tomato paste

1 clove garlic, minced

½ teaspoon salt

½ teaspoon dried oregano leaves

¼ teaspoon ground cumin

¼ teaspoon ground coriander

1. Place chilies in medium bowl; cover with boiling water. Let stand 1 hour.

2. Place chilies along with soaking water in blender; blend until smooth.

3. Whisk together chili mixture and remaining ingredients in medium saucepan. Bring to a boil. Reduce heat. Cover and simmer 10 minutes, stirring occasionally.

Freezer Note

Sauce can be covered and refrigerated up to 3 days
or frozen up to 1 month. Store in resealable plastic freezer bag or
freezer containers with tight-fitting lids.

Roasted Pepper & Tomato Salsa

MAKES 6 CUPS

3 yellow or red bell peppers

2 poblano peppers

1 large onion

2 tablespoons olive oil

4 cloves garlic, minced

1 teaspoon dried oregano leaves

¾ teaspoon salt

½ teaspoon black pepper

2 cans (14½ ounces each) diced tomatoes

¾ cup tomato juice

¼ cup chopped fresh cilantro

1 tablespoon lime juice

1. Preheat oven to 350°F. Chop peppers and onion into ¾-inch pieces. Combine peppers, onion, olive oil, garlic, oregano, salt and black pepper in large bowl; toss to coat. Spread onto two 15×10×1-inch baking pans. Bake 20 minutes or until peppers and onion are lightly browned, stirring after 10 minutes.

2. Combine roasted vegetables and remaining ingredients in large bowl. Spoon into labeled storage containers. Store in refrigerator up to 10 days.

Freezer Note

Salsa can be frozen for up to 2 months. Place individual portions in resealable plastic freezer bag or freezer container with tight-fitting lid. Thaw in refrigerator and stir before serving.

Pork Tenderloin with Red Pepper Sauce

MAKES 1¼ CUPS SAUCE

1 cup chopped onion

¼ cup olive oil

1 cup roasted red peppers, rinsed and drained

¾ cup sour cream

1 packet (1 ounce) HIDDEN VALLEY® The Original Ranch® Salad Dressing & Seasoning Mix

2 pork tenderloins (about 1 pound each), cooked and sliced

Sauté onion in olive oil in a large skillet until soft and lightly browned. Stir in red peppers and heat through. Remove skillet from heat; stir in sour cream and salad dressing & seasoning mix. Transfer warm mixture to food processor and purée until smooth. Serve warm over sliced pork tenderloin.

Serving Suggestion: This sauce is also good served over steak and chicken or used cold as a sandwich spread.

Freezer Note

Use cooked pork tenderloin reserved from Roasted Pork (recipe on following page).

Roasted Pork

MAKES 4 SERVINGS

3 tablespoons barbecue sauce

1 tablespoon reduced-sodium soy sauce

1 tablespoon dry sherry

2 cloves garlic, minced

½ teaspoon crushed Szechwan peppercorns or red pepper flakes

2 whole pork tenderloins (about 1¼ to 1½ pounds total)

1. Preheat oven to 350°F. Combine barbecue sauce, soy sauce, sherry, garlic and peppercorns in small bowl.

2. Brush one-fourth of mixture evenly over each tenderloin. Place on rack in shallow foil-lined roasting pan. Roast 15 minutes; turn and brush with remaining barbecue sauce mixture. Continue to cook until internal temperature reaches 165°F when tested with meat thermometer inserted in thickest part of roast. (Timing will depend on thickness of pork; test at 30 minutes.)

3. Transfer roast to cutting board; cover with foil. Let stand 10 to 15 minutes before carving. Internal temperature will continue to rise 5°F to 10°F during stand time. Slice diagonally and serve warm with rice, if desired.

Variation: For Chinese Barbecued Pork, add 1 teaspoon red food coloring to barbecue sauce mixture. Prepare tenderloins as recipe directs. Tenderloins can be grilled over medium coals until an internal temperature of 155°F is reached. (Turn pork after 8 minutes; check temperature at 16 minutes.)

Freezer Note

For use in other recipes, cut into portions and refrigerate up to 3 days or freeze up to 3 months. Overwrap portions in plastic wrap, and store in resealable plastic freezer bag.

Oriental Fried Rice

MAKES 6 SERVINGS

3 cups cooked brown rice, cold

½ cup slivered cooked roast pork

½ cup finely chopped celery

½ cup fresh bean sprouts*

⅓ cup sliced green onions

1 egg, beaten
 Vegetable cooking spray

¼ teaspoon black pepper

2 tablespoons soy sauce

Substitute canned bean sprouts, rinsed and drained, for fresh, if desired.

Combine rice, pork, celery, bean sprouts, onions, and egg in large skillet coated with cooking spray. Cook, stirring, 3 minutes over high heat. Add pepper and soy sauce. Cook, stirring, 1 minute longer.

To microwave: Combine rice, pork, celery, bean sprouts, and onions in shallow 2-quart microproof baking dish coated with cooking spray. Cook on HIGH 2 to 3 minutes. Add egg, pepper, and soy sauce. Cook on HIGH 1 to 2 minutes or until egg is set, stirring to separate grains.

Tip: When preparing fried rice, always begin with cold rice. The grains separate better if cold and it's a great way to use leftover rice.

Speed it up: Use cooked pork tenderloin reserved from Roasted Pork (recipe on page 83).

*Favorite recipe from **USA Rice***

Freezer Note

When you cook rice, make a double batch and freeze the extra rice flat in resealable plastic freezer bags for later use.

Sesame Pork Salad

- 3 cups cooked rice
- 1½ cups slivered cooked pork*
- ¼ pound fresh snow peas, trimmed and julienned
- 1 medium cucumber, peeled, seeded and julienned
- 1 medium red bell pepper, julienned
- ½ cup sliced green onions
- 2 tablespoons sesame seeds, toasted (optional)
- ¼ cup chicken broth
- 3 tablespoons rice or white wine vinegar
- 3 tablespoons soy sauce
- 1 tablespoon peanut oil
- 1 teaspoon sesame oil

*Substitute 1½ cups slivered cooked chicken for pork, if desired.

Combine rice, pork, snow peas, cucumber, bell pepper, onions and sesame seeds in large bowl. Combine broth, vinegar, soy sauce and oils in small jar with lid; shake well. Pour over rice mixture; toss lightly. Serve at room temperature or slightly chilled.

Speed it up: Use cooked pork tenderloin reserved from Roasted Pork (recipe on page 83).

*Favorite recipe from **USA Rice***

Freezer Note

When you cook rice, make a double batch and freeze the extra rice flat in resealable plastic freezer bags for later use.

Crispy Roasted Chicken

MAKES 8 TO 10 SERVINGS

1 **roasting chicken or capon (about 6½ pounds)**

1 **tablespoon peanut or vegetable oil**
2 **cloves garlic, minced**
1 **tablespoon soy sauce**

1. Preheat oven to 350°F. Rinse chicken; pat dry. Place on rack in shallow, foil-lined roasting pan.

2. Combine oil and garlic in small cup; brush evenly over chicken. Roast 15 to 20 minutes per pound or until internal temperature reaches 170°F when tested with meat thermometer inserted in thickest part of thigh not touching bone.

3. Increase oven temperature to 450°F. Remove drippings from pan; discard. Brush chicken evenly with soy sauce. Roast 5 to 10 minutes until skin is very crisp and deep golden brown. Transfer chicken to cutting board; let stand 10 to 15 minutes before carving. Internal temperature will continue to rise 5°F to 10°F during stand time. Cover and refrigerate leftovers up to 3 days.

Freezer Note

For use in other recipes, cut into portions and refrigerate up to 3 days or freeze up to 3 months. Overwrap individual portions in plastic wrap, and store in resealable plastic freezer bag or freezer container with tight-fitting lid.

Chicken Enchilada Skillet Casserole

MAKES 4 SERVINGS

1 bag (16 ounces) BIRDS EYE® frozen Farm Fresh Mixtures Broccoli, Corn & Red Peppers

3 cups shredded cooked chicken

1 can (16 ounces) diced tomatoes, undrained

1 package (1¼ ounces) taco seasoning mix

1 cup shredded Monterey Jack cheese

8 ounces tortilla chips

• In large skillet, combine vegetables, chicken, tomatoes and seasoning mix; bring to boil over medium-high heat.

• Cover; cook 4 minutes or until vegetables are cooked and mixture is heated through.

• Sprinkle with cheese; cover and cook 2 minutes more or until cheese is melted.

• Serve with chips.

Freezer Note

Use cooked chicken reserved from Crispy Roasted Chicken (recipe on previous page) or Classic Matzoh Ball Soup (recipe on page 90).

Ranch-Up!™ Pizza

MAKES 8 SERVINGS

½ cup Wish-Bone® Ranch Up!™ Zesty, Classic or Cheesy Dressing

1 (12-inch) pre-baked pizza crust

1 cup cooked chicken, cubed

1 medium tomato, sliced and quartered

1 cup shredded Monterey Jack or mozzarella cheese (about 4 ounces)

1 green onion, sliced

- Preheat oven to 450°F.
- Evenly spread Ranch-Up!™ on crust.
- Top with chicken, tomato, cheese and green onion.
- Season, if desired, with salt and ground black pepper.
- Bake 10 minutes or until heated through and cheese is melted.

Tropical Chicken Salad

MAKES 4 SERVINGS

Tropical Salad Dressing (recipe follows)

3 cups cubed cooked chicken

¾ cup coarsely chopped celery

¾ cup seedless red or green grape halves

¾ cup coarsely chopped macadamia nuts or toasted almonds

Lettuce leaves

Strawberries and kiwifruit for garnish

Toasted flaked coconut for garnish*

*To toast coconut, spread evenly on ungreased cookie sheet. Toast in preheated 350°F oven 5 to 7 minutes, stirring occasionally until light golden brown.

Tropical Chicken Salad

Prepare Tropical Salad Dressing. Combine chicken, celery, grapes and nuts in large bowl; stir in 1 cup dressing. Cover; refrigerate 1 hour. Mound chicken salad on lettuce-lined platter or individual plates. Garnish with strawberries, kiwifruit and coconut. Serve with remaining dressing.

Tropical Salad Dressing: Place ½ cup cream of coconut, ⅓ cup red wine vinegar, 1 teaspoon dry mustard, 1 teaspoon salt and 1 clove peeled garlic in blender or food processor container. With processor on, slowly add 1 cup vegetable oil in thin stream, processing until smooth.

Freezer Note

Use cooked chicken reserved from Crispy Roasted Chicken (recipe on page 86) or Classic Matzoh Ball Soup (recipe on page 90).

Classic Matzoh Ball Soup

MAKES 6 SERVINGS

- 1 whole chicken (about 3½ pounds), cut into serving pieces
- 7 cups plus 2 tablespoons water, divided
- 3 carrots, cut into 1-inch pieces
- 3 ribs celery, cut into 1-inch pieces
- 1 medium onion, unpeeled, quartered
- 1 large parsnip, cut into 1-inch pieces (optional)
- 1 head garlic, separated into cloves, unpeeled

- 3 sprigs parsley
- 8 to 10 whole black peppercorns
- 4 eggs
- 1 cup matzoh meal
- ¼ cup parve margarine, melted, cooled
- 1 tablespoon grated onion
- ½ teaspoon salt
- ⅛ teaspoon ground white pepper or ¼ teaspoon freshly ground black pepper

Chopped fresh parsley, for garnish

Combine chicken and 7 cups water in Dutch oven. Bring to a boil over medium heat. Remove any foam from surface of water with large metal spoon; discard. Add carrots, celery, unpeeled onion, parsnip, garlic, parsley and whole peppercorns. Cover; simmer 3 hours or until chicken is no longer pink in center. Remove from heat; cool 30 minutes. Strain soup; reserve chicken and broth separately. Discard vegetables. Remove skin and bones from chicken; discard.* Reserve chicken for another use.

Beat eggs in large bowl on medium speed of electric mixer. Add matzoh meal, margarine, remaining 2 tablespoons water, grated onion, salt and ground pepper. Mix at low speed until well blended. Let stand 15 to 30 minutes. With wet hands, form matzoh mixture into 12 (2-inch) balls.

Bring 8 cups water to a boil in Dutch oven. Drop matzoh balls, one at a time, into boiling water. Reduce heat. Cover; simmer 35 to 40 minutes or until matzoh balls are cooked through. Drain well.

Add reserved broth to Dutch oven. Bring to a boil over high heat. Add salt to taste. Reduce heat; cover. Simmer 5 minutes or until matzoh balls are heated through. Garnish with parsley, if desired.

Favorite recipe from **Hebrew National®**

*Chicken and broth may be covered and refrigerated up to 3 days or frozen up to 3 months.

Freezer Note

Package and freeze chicken and broth separately. Broth can be frozen in freezer containers for several months; measure in 1- or 2-cup portions for use in other recipes. Or, freeze broth in ice cube trays, pouring 1 fluid ounce into each section. Then, release cubes and store in resealable plastic freezer bag.

Black Bean Soup

MAKES 10 SERVINGS

2 tablespoons vegetable oil

1 large onion, chopped

3 large cloves garlic, minced

4 cans (15 to 19 ounces each) black beans, undrained

2 cans (14½ ounces each) reduced-sodium chicken broth

⅓ cup *Frank's® RedHot®* Original Cayenne Pepper Sauce

¼ cup minced fresh cilantro

2 teaspoons ground cumin

1. Heat oil in 4- to 5-quart saucepan. Add onion and garlic; cook until tender. Stir in beans with liquid, broth, *Frank's RedHot* Sauce, cilantro and cumin.

2. Bring to a boil. Reduce heat; simmer, partially covered, 30 minutes, stirring often.

3. Remove 1 cup soup. Place in blender; cover securely and process until smooth. Return to saucepan; stir. Serve soup in individual soup bowls. Top with dollop of sour cream, if desired.

Freezer Note

This soup freezes well. Freeze in individual portions in resealable plastic freezer bag or freezer container with tight-fitting lid. Thaw and reheat in microwave oven. If available, use chicken broth reserved from Classic Matzoh Ball Soup (recipe on page 90).

Baked Bean Stew.........................42
Baked French Toast Wedges........12
Barbecue Dipping Sauce.............32
Basic Browned Ground Beef........78
Basic White Bread......................70
Beef and Pasta Soup 56
Beef Enchiladas.........................48
Beef Stock 57
Black Bean Soup 92
Breakfast Cookies 22
Breakfast in a Cup......................24
Broccoli-Cheese Quesadillas.......37

California Chicken Pot Pies...........44
Caribbean Chicken
    Quesadillas...............................36
Chicken Enchilada
    Skillet Casserole 87
Chicken Nuggets with
    Barbecue Dipping Sauce 32
Classic Matzoh Ball Soup.............90
Cousin Arlene's
    Spaghetti Lasagna.....................54
Creamy Oatmeal.........................20
Crispy Roasted Chicken...............86

Easy Chicken and
    Mushroom Stroganoff 50
Egg and Sausage
    Breakfast Strudel 60

Freezer Buttermilk Biscuits 69
Freezer Rolls...............................72

Ham and Swiss Quiche.................30
Hearty Chili 40
Hearty Chili Seasoning Mix 41
Homemade Sausage Patties 20

Jamaican Meat Patties..................28

Make-Ahead Dill Chicken
    in Foil 58
Meal in a Bun 26
Mediterranean Microwave
    Meat Loaf 67

Mini-Quiche Appetizers................30
Mixed Berry Topping 14
Mixed Fruit Topping 13

Oat and Apple Granola 24
Oriental Fried Rice 84

Peachy Keen Topping...................13
Peachy Oat Bran Muffins 16
Pecan Sticky Buns 62
Pizza Filling................................26
Pizza Turnovers...........................34
Pizza-Style Stuffed Potatoes 64
Pork Tenderloin with
    Red Pepper Sauce.....................82

Ranch-Up!™ Pizza 88
Red Chili Sauce...........................80
Red Pepper Sauce 82
Rise and Shine Sausage
    Oatmeal Cups 18
Roasted Pepper & Tomato
    Salsa..81
Roasted Pork...............................83

Sausage Pinwheels 68
Savory Onion Cheese Tart...........38
Sesame Pork Salad 85
Silver Dollar Pancakes with
    Mixed Berry Topping.................14
Southwestern Turkey
    Empanadas...............................66
Spaghetti Bolognese 76
Strawberry Topping 13
Stuffed Cabbage Rolls..................46
Stuffed Green Peppers 46
Swedish Meatballs.......................52

Tortellini Bake Parmesano 74
Tostado Filling............................26
Tropical Chicken Salad.................88
Tropical Salad Dressing 89

Veg•All® Beef Chili.......................79

Waffles......................................10

ACKNOWLEDGMENTS

The publisher would like to thank the companies and organizations listed below for the use of their recipes and photographs in this publication.

◆

ACH FOOD COMPANIES, INC.

American Dry Bean Board

American Lamb Council

Bays English Muffin Corporation

Birds Eye® Foods

Bob Evans®

CanolaInfo.

Crisco is a registered trademark of
The J.M. Smucker Company

Del Monte Corporation

Egg Beaters®

Fleischmann's Yeast

Hebrew National®

The Hidden Valley® Food Products Company

Jennie-O Turkey Store®

National Chicken Council/US Poultry & Egg Association

Nestlé USA

North Dakota Wheat Commission

Reckitt Benckiser Inc.

Unilever Foods North America

USA Rice Federation

Veg•All®